"I am so excited about this book! Our singing of the Lord shapes who we are more than we often know, and Fanny Crosby's deep joy dances towards each new generation through the song of her writing and the song of her life. Her voice helped me find mine."

KRISTYN GETTY, Author, Lyricist and Worship Leader

"The wonderful storytelling and charming illustrations make the mini-biographies in this series pitch-perfect for even the youngest readers."

CHAMP THORNTON, Author, *The Radical Book for Kids*

"A wonderful series, beautifully illustrated, introducing your children to godly women."

BLAIR LINNE, Spoken Word Artist

thegoodbook
for children

Fanny Crosby
© Laura Caputo-Wickham / The Good Book Company 2022.
Reprinted 2024.

Illustrated by Jess Rose | Design and Art Direction by André Parker

Photograph source (p 22): Fanny J. Crosby, Memories of Eighty Years (Boston, MA: James H. Earle & Co., 1906). Now Public Domain.

"The Good Book For Children" is an imprint of The Good Book Company Ltd thegoodbook.com | thegoodbook.co.uk | thegoodbook.com.au thegoodbook.co.nz | thegoodbook.co.in

ISBN: 9781784987473 | JOB-007686 | Printed in India

Do Great Things for God

Fanny Crosby

The Girl Who Couldn't See but Helped the World to Sing

Laura Caputo-Wickham

Illustrated by Jess Rose

Baby Frances – or Fanny, as everyone called her – was only six weeks old when she became blind. One day she could see, and the next...

... she couldn't.

But she could still *feel* the warmth of her mummy's cuddles and *smell* her nice perfume. She could *hear* her sisters singing and *taste* the sweetness of fruit.

And that, for Fanny, was enough.

Because not only was Fanny a happy girl, always looking for reasons to be thankful; she was also extremely, incredibly, amazingly...

... smart!

By the age of ten, Fanny had already memorised eight books of the Bible. She could knit, climb, play sports and write poetry.

"What a pity you can't see," people often said.
But Fanny wouldn't have had it any other way.

"The first thing my eyes will ever see will be
the face of Jesus in heaven," she'd reply.
And this filled her with joy.

When Fanny was offered a place at a school for blind children in New York, she was thrilled! And though she missed her family, she enjoyed being with other children like herself.

Together, they'd get up to all sorts of mischief, like the night they sneaked into the school's fruit-and-vegetable garden for a cheeky midnight snack.

At school, Fanny practised her poetry and wrote beautiful verses that she shared with her family and friends.

"You're such a great poet, Fanny!" they'd say.

Then, one night,
she had a dream.

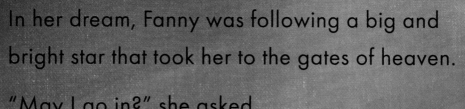

In her dream, Fanny was following a big and bright star that took her to the gates of heaven.

"May I go in?" she asked.

"Not yet, Fanny," a voice replied.

"But I will open the gates, just a little, so that you can hear one burst of eternal music."

That's when Fanny heard the most beautiful sound that her ears had ever heard. Not long after that, she began writing songs about God.

And what wonderful songs she wrote!

Her hymns helped many people to feel closer to God and were so popular that she soon found herself writing six or seven a day!

But every time, before even starting, Fanny would stop and pray, asking for God's help.

Sometimes, Fanny wrote the words first,
which would then be turned into music.
Other times, it went the other way round.

One day, a friend played a tune and asked, "What do you think it says, Fanny?"

"Blessed assurance, Jesus is mine," she replied.

And, just like that, one of her most famous hymns was born – a hymn that tells us that there's great happiness (or *blessing*) in knowing for sure (having *assurance*) that Jesus loves us and is with us.

Another day, a musician knocked on Fanny's door.

"Help me, Fanny!" he said. "I've written the music; can you write the words? And could you do it quickly? I have a train to catch."

He hummed the tune, and Fanny wrote the hymn "Safe in the Arms of Jesus" in just 15 minutes!

Safe in the arms of Jesus

Fanny loved to write songs about Jesus. This one tells us that because Jesus is so kind, his friends don't need to be scared of anything.

When asked how many hymns she'd written in her lifetime, Fanny would mull it over and say,

"Over five thousand".

She lived a busy and long life – "a life of joy and sunshine", as she liked to describe it.

"Serve the LORD with gladness," says Psalm 100 v 2; "come before him with joyful songs".

And that's exactly what Fanny did.

Right until the end.

And over 100 years later, we still sing her songs, knowing that Fanny is now safe in the arms of Jesus.

Fanny Crosby

1820 – 1915

"Serve the LORD with gladness;
come before him with joyful songs."
Psalm 100 v 2

Questions to Think About

1. Which part of Fanny's story did you like best?

2. Look up one of the songs written by Fanny. Sing along if you can. Do you have a favourite Christian song? Why do you like it best?

3. What did Fanny say when people thought it was a pity that she was blind? Fanny knew that being with Jesus in heaven would be wonderful. What are you particularly looking forward to about heaven?

4. What ideas does Fanny's story give you about how you might serve Jesus when you are older?

5. What is one truth about God that you'd like to remember from this story?

Fanny Crosby

24th March 1820 Frances Jane Crosby was born to John and Mercy Crosby in Putnam County, New York, USA.

   Many think that her blindness was the result of bad advice given by an unexperienced doctor when Fanny suffered from an infection as a baby.

   When she was only six months old, her father died, and Fanny was raised by her mother and her grandmother, Eunice, who would read her the Bible and answer her many questions.

1828 By the age of eight, Fanny had written her first poem:

> *Oh, what a happy child I am,*
> *Although I cannot see!*
> *I am resolved that in this world*
> *Contented I will be.*
> *How many blessings I enjoy*
> *That other people don't!*
> *So weep or sigh because I'm blind,*
> *I cannot, nor I won't!*

1835 Though Fanny loved learning, she couldn't get the support she needed from her school at home so, at the age of 15, she entered what was then known as the New York Institution for the Blind. It was during her years there that Fanny's talent as a poet was discovered.

1858 Fanny married Alexander Van Alstyne, a musician who, like her, was also blind. The two met in the school where Fanny was working as a teacher. Alexander, or "Van", as everyone called him, set some of Fanny's hymns to music.

1864 A famous hymn writer called William B. Bradbury asked Fanny to write hymns for him. That's when Fanny's busy career took off. Her name appeared in hymn books so many times that she often signed her songs using made-up names like "Ella Dale", "Julia Stirling", "Charles Burns" and more.

During her life, Fanny met many important people, from famous singers to the president of the United States, Grover Cleveland.

12th February 1915 Fanny died at the age of 95.

It's hard to know exactly how many hymns she wrote in total, but many believe it's around 9,000. Some of these have been translated into different languages and are still sung today.

Among her most famous hymns, there are
"Pass Me Not, O Gentle Saviour",
"Blessed Assurance",
"To God Be the Glory", and
"Safe in the Arms of Jesus".

NORTH
AMERICA

USA

SOUTH
AMERICA

EU

World Map

Where in the world
did Fanny's story
take place?

Interact With Fanny's Story!

's

Family Project: The New York Institute for Special Education (NYISE)

God made Fanny Crosby with some really amazing talents and abilities. He also made her without the ability to see, which is called "blind." Fanny attended school at the New York Institution for the Blind, now known as The New York Institute for Special Education (NYISE). Read Psalm 139 v 13 together and talk about how God makes us in his image. Then, read 1 Corinthians 15 v 35–44 and discuss how Christians will receive new bodies in the new creation.

Day 1: Overview

- Locate NYISE on a map.
- How many students attend NYISE?

- What is the NYISE mission?

Day 2: NYISE History

- When was the NYISE founded?

- When did the name of the school change from the New York Institution for the Blind to The New York Institute for Special Education?

- When did the NYISE rowing program begin?

Day 5: Ministries

- How does *Special Touch Ministries* serve people who are blind or have limited eyesight?

- How does *Christian Blind Mission International* (CBM) serve people who are blind or limited eyesight?

- How can you help to serve those in your church and community who are blind or have limited eyesight?

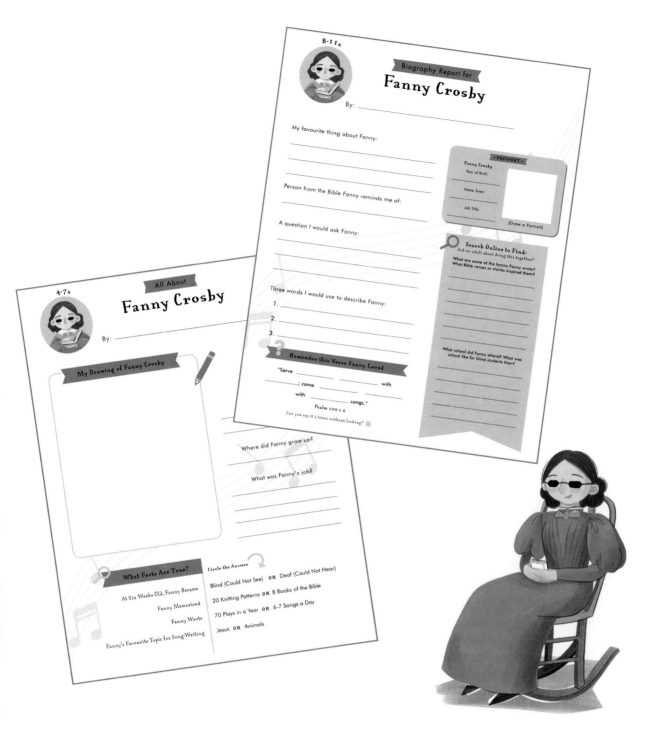

8-11s

Biography Report for
Fanny Crosby

By: _____

My favourite thing about Fanny:

_____

_____

Person from the Bible Fanny reminds me of:

_____

A question I would ask Fanny:

_____

_____

Three words I would use to describe Fanny:

1. _____

2. _____

3. _____

· PASSPORT ·

Fanny Crosby

Year of Birth:

Home Town:

Job Title:

[Draw a Portrait]

Search Online to Find:
Ask an adult about doing this together!

What are some of the hymns Fanny wrote?
What Bible verses or stories inspired them?

_____

_____

_____

What school did Fanny attend? What was
school like for blind students then?

_____

_____

Remember this Verse Fanny Loved

"Serve _____ with

_____; come _____ with

_____ songs."

Psalm 100 v 2

Can you say it 5 times without looking? ☐

4-7s

All About
Fanny Crosby

By: _____

My Drawing of Fanny Crosby

Where did Fanny grow up?

_____

What was Fanny's job?

_____

_____

What Facts Are True? Circle the Answer

At Six Weeks Old, Fanny Became   Blind (Could Not See) OR Deaf (Could Not Hear)

Fanny Memorized   20 Knitting Patterns OR 8 Books of the Bible

Fanny Wrote   70 Plays in a Year OR 6-7 Songs a Day

Fanny's Favourite Topic for Song-Writing   Jesus OR Animals

Download Free Resources at

thegoodbook.com/kids-resources

Do Great Things for God

Inspiring Biographies for Young Children

Corrie ten Boom
The Courageous Woman and the Secret Room
Laura Caputo-Wickham
Illustrated by Isabel Muñoz

Betsey Stockton
The Girl With a Missionary Dream
Laura Caputo-Wickham
Illustrated by Eunji Jung

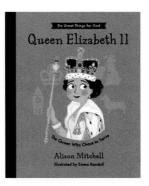

Queen Elizabeth II
The Queen Who Chose to Serve
Alison Mitchell
Illustrated by Emma Randall

Helen Roseveare
The Doctor Who Kept Going No Matter What
Laura Caputo-Wickham
Illustrated by Cecilia Messina

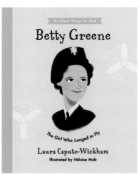

Gladys Aylward
The Little Woman With a Big Dream
Laura Caputo-Wickham
Illustrated by Jess Rose

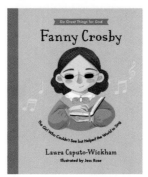

Betty Greene
The Girl Who Longed to Fly
Laura Caputo-Wickham
Illustrated by Héloïse Mab

Fanny Crosby
The Girl Who Couldn't See but Helped the World to Sing
Laura Caputo-Wickham
Illustrated by Jess Rose

Fannie Lou Hamer
That Courageous Woman Who Marched for Dignity
K. A. Ellis
Illustrated by Shiri Maeng

Maria Fearing
The Girl Who Dreamed of Distant Lands
K. A. Ellis
Illustrated by Isabel Muñoz

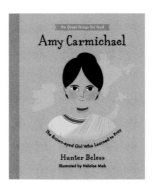

Amy Carmichael
The Brown-eyed Girl Who Learned to Pray
Hunter Beless
Illustrated by Héloïse Mab

Susannah Spurgeon
The Pastor's Wife Who Didn't Let Sickness Stop Her
Mary K. Mohler
Illustrated by Cecilia Messina